THE DAY MY FART FOLLOWED ME HOME

Ben Jackson & Sam Lawrence

INDIE
Publishing
— GROUP —

www.indiepublishinggroup.com

This is for all those parents who just need to giggle with their kids sometimes.

Timmy was walking home from school when he had a feeling he was being followed.

"What are you?" Timmy asked, looking at the furry little green creature in front of him.

"I'm your little fart!" the little fart blurted out excitedly.

"**You're my what?**" Timmy exclaimed.

"**You heard me right!**" the creature giggled, leaping down from the tree stump. He pointed a stubby green finger at Timmy.

"**We are going to be best friends forever!**" Little Fart giggled again as he jumped up and down.

Timmy was getting a little bit concerned now. What if someone saw him walking home with a furry little green creature that smelled funny? What if they smelled it?

"You can't follow me home!" Timmy blurted out, panicking.

"Why not? You always leave me behind and run away. Well, not today! Now we can be best friends forever!" Little Fart replied, brushing up against Timmy's leg.

"But, umm...what if someone sees you?" Timmy asked.

"Well, they can't see me, silly. Only you can," Little Fart replied.

"Okay, well, that's not too bad," said Timmy, breathing a huge sigh of relief.

"**But they can smell me. No one else can see me, but everyone can smell me,**" Little Fart said, beaming proudly. He was glad to be helping Timmy learn all about little farts.

"**Oh no! They will think I have farted everywhere I go!**" Timmy shouted, holding his hands over his face. Timmy was really starting to sweat now. His whole life could be ruined by one little fart.

Timmy decided he had to get away from the strange, smelly little creature. He broke into a sprint, not bothering to stop and look back. He just ran. He ran into his house, slamming the front door loudly behind him.

"Hi, Mom," Timmy blurted in between gasps, as he ran up the stairs. This was no time to stop for small talk. He shut himself in his bedroom and struggled to catch his breath.

"**Boo!**" an excited little voice shouted from beside him. "**Surprised to see me?**" Little Fart asked.

"**Oh, my!**" Timmy cried, almost falling off his bed with surprise. "**How did you get here?**" Timmy asked looking around his room.

"That was fast running! Can we do it again?" Little Fart asked.

How on earth did he do that? Timmy wondered, scratching his head, perplexed by this small green creature so determined to be his friend.

Timmy sighed and looked at Little Fart sitting next to him. *I suppose he isn't that bad,* Timmy thought.

"Okay, if we are going to be friends, then we need to make some rules," Timmy said, scratching his head in thought.

"Sure! We will be friends forever!" Little Fart shouted, jumping up and down. Then he hugged Timmy excitedly.

"Okay, okay!" Timmy laughed as he hugged Little Fart back. Perhaps having a secret friend to talk to wouldn't be such a bad thing, even if he was a bit clingy...and smelly.

"Okay, Little Fart, but we need some ground rules. Rule one: keep your distance when I'm around other people. Just stay a little bit away...so they don't smell you, okay?"

"Sure, that's easy! I'm used to staying out of people's way," Little Fart replied happily.

"Rule two: when I go to school, you need to stay at home, so the teachers and kids don't smell you. I don't want my classroom smelling like a little fart all day," Timmy said.

"Rule three: you need to stay out of Mom's way. She already thinks I smell. I don't want to have to take any more baths!"

"Yep, yep, sure. No stinky classrooms. Oh boy, oh boy! We are going to be best friends forever!" Little Fart shouted, jumping all around Timmy again.

"Sure! I guess we are!" From that day on, the two were indeed the best of friends, just a little boy and his Little Fart, taking on the world.

Check out what Timmy and Little Fart get up to next!

Note From The Authors

As Indie authors, we work hard to produce high-quality work for the enjoyment of all our readers. If you can spare one minute, please leave a review of our book. We would greatly appreciate it! Let everyone know just how much you and your children enjoyed Timmy and his Fart! We are currently working on expanding this series, so stay tuned for future updates by following us on Amazon. Check out our Facebook page or website for more updates.

www.facebook.com/benandsamauthors & www.benandsamauthors.com

Thank you, Ben and Sam ☺

About the Authors

Ben and Sam currently live in Ontario, Canada, and Tasmania, Australia. Ben was born in Tasmania, Australia, while Sam was born in Toronto, Canada. Between the two of them, they enjoy travelling frequently, and they both have two children. With their three boys and one girl, they both enjoy spending quality time with their families, reading books, playing games, and exploring both Canada and Australia.

Other Books by Ben & Sam

My Little Fart Series

The Day My Fart Followed Me Home
The Day My Fart Followed Me To Hockey
The Day My Fart Followed Santa Up The Chimney
The Day My Fart Followed Me To Soccer
The Day My Fart Followed Me To The Dentist
The Day My Fart Followed Me To The Zoo
The Day My Fart Followed Me To Baseball
The Day My Fart Followed Me To The Hospital
It's Not Easy Being A Little Fart

If I Was A Caterpillar
Don't Fart in the Pool

Hockey Wars Series

Hockey Wars
Hockey Wars 2 - The New Girl
Hockey Wars 3 - The Tournament
Hockey Wars 4 - Championships
Hockey Wars 5 - Lacrosse Wars
Hockey Wars 6 - Middle School
Hockey Wars 7 - Winter Break
Hockey Wars 8 - Spring Break
Hockey Wars 9 - Summer Camp
Hockey Wars 10 - State Tryouts
Hockey Wars 11 - State Tournament
Hockey Wars 12 - Euro Tournament

Manufactured by Amazon.ca
Bolton, ON

PRAISE FOR
OVER THE BEACH